Under Pressure
The Science of Stress

Tanya Lloyd Kyi

Marie-Ève Tremblay

For my family, who love me even when I'm stressed — T.L.K.

Acknowledgments

Thank you to Laura Chiarenza for her wisdom and expertise, and to the team at
Kids Can Press for being generally fabulous. You made the creation of this book entirely un-stressful.
Thank you also to researchers such as Yoshifumi Miyazaki, who dedicated years to finding ways for us to
decrease stress and anxiety. And apologies to my son, who now has to take long walks in the woods
with his family when he'd rather be playing video games.

Kids Can Press gratefully acknowledges the financial
support of the Government of Ontario, through
Ontario Creates; the Ontario Arts Council; the Canada
Council for the Arts; and the Government of Canada
for our publishing activity.

Published in Canada and the U.S. by Kids Can Press Ltd.
25 Dockside Drive, Toronto, ON M5A 0B5

Kids Can Press is a Corus Entertainment Inc. company

www.kidscanpress.com

The artwork in this book was rendered digitally in
Photoshop.
The text is set in Picadilly.

Edited by Jennifer Stokes
Designed by Marie Bartholomew

Printed and bound in Shenzhen, China, in 3/2019 by
C&C Offset

CM 19 0 9 8 7 6 5 4 3 2 1

Library and Archives Canada Cataloguing in Publication

Kyi, Tanya Lloyd, 1973–, author
  Under pressure : the science of stress / Tanya Lloyd Kyi,
Marie-Ève Tremblay.

ISBN 978-1-5253-0007-3 (hardcover)

    1. Stress (Physiology) — Juvenile literature. 2.
Stress (Psychology) — Juvenile literature. I. Tremblay,
Marie-Ève, 1978 July 19–, illustrator II. Title.

QP82.2.S8K95 2019   j616.9'8   C2018-905843-9

Contents

Introduction:
The Sticks and Stones of Stress **4**

Chapter 1:
Fight, Flight or Freeze **6**

Chapter 2:
The Long Game **18**

Chapter 3:
Bounce Back **30**

Chapter 4:
Helpful Highs **44**

Chapter 5:
Tension Tamers **56**

Conclusion:
Personal Space **68**

Further Reading **70**

Selected Sources **70**

Index **75**

Introduction

The Sticks and Stones of Stress

As the morning bell rings and the principal stalks the hallway, you frantically rummage through your locker. Binders and papers fly to the floor behind you.

"She's lost her history report," whispers one of your friends.

"And her dog's at the vet," says another.

"She's a wreck."

"A total basket case."

We tend to view stress as a bad thing, and the names we use for it aren't particularly nice. *Frazzled. Flustered. Freaking out.* But we've all experienced that sweaty, heart-racing, under-pressure feeling. It's not something we can avoid or escape. The roots of stress go back millions of years, to when early humans loped through the savanna, fighting hyenas and fleeing lions. The emergency-action hormones and chemicals in our bodies evolved to help us deal with danger.

And if we feel stress in our school hallways, far from the dangers of the savanna, we shouldn't be too hard on ourselves. We all juggle commitments and responsibilities. We manage math tests, friendship fractures and family emergencies. We have days when we're calm and days when we're anxious.

We're still learning to adapt those early brain responses to the technology and traffic of modern life. Scientists are learning, too. Each year, they discover new information about how our brains grow and change, and how we react to the demands of the world around us.

This book explores the science of anxiety and the history of stress research. It examines the effects of pressure on the human body and what we can do about them. The book also includes some wacky historical beliefs, strange experiments and stories of stressed-out stress researchers.

In the following chapters, you'll learn about the fight-or-flight reaction to sudden danger, how people cope with chronic pressure, how trauma can affect the brain, the ways athletes put pressure to work and the surprising treatments scientists have found for stress in our everyday lives.

At the end of it all, you might be less willing to call yourself a wreck, and more likely to admire how well your body and brain work together. When the going gets rough … that's when your toughest parts get going.

Chapter 1

Fight, Flight or Freeze

You stroll home from school, kicking a pebble as you go. At the corner by the coffee shop, you absentmindedly step into the crosswalk and ...

Danger!

Tires screech. A horn blasts. Before your brain has even formed the words *city bus*, you've leaped out of the way. You sprint the last few steps to the curb, where you lean on your knees, gasping.

Your whole body's shaking. Your heart pounds, your ears ring and all you can see is the afterimage of that big bus fender bearing down on you.

You've experienced something called the fight-or-flight response. In its most basic form, stress is your body's reaction to danger. In a crisis, you instinctively decide whether to fight or — in this case — run away.

Your reactions to an oncoming bus are exactly the same as your ancestors' reactions to an encounter with a lion. Our bodies have been practicing the emergency stress response for millions of years.

X-Ray Vision

How did stress research begin?

With cat food.

In the early 1900s, a Harvard Medical School professor named Walter Cannon was studying digestion. He mixed cat food with a chemical dye, then used X-rays to trace the substance as it moved through kitty bellies.

Walter noticed something strange. If a cat was upset, or startled by a sudden noise, all digestion stopped. It seemed as if the cat's emotions were affecting its insides.

Walter shifted the entire focus of his research. He began studying the way animals, including humans, react to sudden stimuli. Over time, he learned that when an animal is frightened, the body stops spending energy on everyday things like digestion and shifts into an emergency-response mode.

Walter wrote a book about the "fight instinct" and the "flight instinct." He suggested that when we're startled, we instantly decide either to battle or to run. Both reactions are triggered by fear, and both affect many systems of the body.

Other researchers called Walter's discovery the "fight-or-flight response." And the science of stress was born.

Today, scientists have added a third possible response to crisis: freeze. There are times when that saber-toothed cat is a little too close. We don't have time to run, and we'll never win the fight. So our brains tell us to do what a chameleon might: freeze, and hope to blend in with the trees.

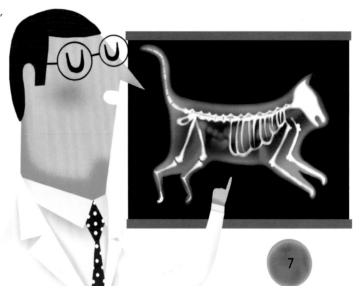

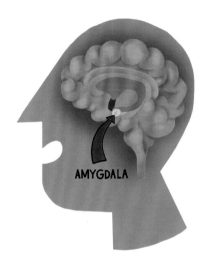

AMYGDALA

Amygdalae, which is the plural form of *amygdala*, comes from the Greek word for almonds. They're our almond-shaped control pods.

The word *stress* itself was first used by physicists to describe pressure. For example, leaning against a fence puts stress on the wood. In the 1920s, a University of Montreal doctor named Hans Selye began using the word to describe the feelings of hospital patients. No matter what was physically wrong with them, they all seemed to be experiencing strain, or pressure. Like the wooden fence, they were under stress.

Hans had other ideas, too. He noticed the fight-or-flight response could be triggered by good events as well as bad. Imagine a group of people leaping from behind your living room couch and yelling, "Surprise!" Your hands fly into the air and your heart races. For a second, you feel like running away. Your body is responding to stress, even though a birthday party's usually a good thing.

Many of our fight-or-flight reflexes stem from the amygdalae — two small regions near the base of the brain. People often call this region the "reptilian brain" because it prompts some of our most basic drives and instincts. In 2011, scientists in California wrote about a woman called S.M. (They identified her by initials only for privacy reasons.) She had damaged her amygdalae twenty years before. The scientists took S.M. into a pet store full of snakes and spiders. They walked her through a haunted house, then they showed her scary movies. S.M. displayed no fear. This helped prove to scientists that the amygdalae were definitely part of the brain's emergency-response system.

During an intense situation, the brain's big thinking center — the prefrontal cortex — gets overwhelmed. And that's okay, because a crisis is no time to ponder flowcharts or debate philosophies. When our eyes or ears sense danger, the brain passes that information directly to our amygdalae. Jump first; think later!

What's Shaking?

Introducing the big boss: your autonomic nervous system. It takes care of all those things you don't think about, like the beating of your heart and the wriggling of your intestines.

Like any big boss, your autonomic nervous system has workers. It puts two of them in charge of stress. The first is the sympathetic nervous system, manager of emergency responses. When a bus looms or a tiger attacks, the sympathetic nervous system makes instant changes. It cues the adrenal glands, near the kidneys, to produce three stress hormones: adrenaline, norepinephrine and cortisol. These chemicals take care of most of your fight-or-flight necessities. When you get a blast of them, here's what happens:

- Your arms shoot up, ready for defense.
- Your heart races, sending extra blood to your muscles and your brain (and away from your digestive system, as Walter Cannon discovered).
- Your breathing speeds up so you get extra oxygen.

Book Smarts

Though scientists didn't understand the fight-or-flight response until the early 1900s, novelists have been describing it for ages. The world's first-known adventure novel, *Sinuhe*, was written in Egypt almost four thousand years ago. In it, the narrator says: "Confused by fear was my heart, both my arms extended, a shaking was falling on all my limbs." That author didn't need science experiments to understand the effects of stress.

- Your pupils dilate so you can see more clearly.
- The tiny blood vessels in your skin shrink so you won't bleed as quickly.
- Your immune system leaps into high gear in case of injury.
- Your brain turns down your pain receptors so you can fight even if you're hurt.

All of that happens before you've even had time to say, "Get me out of here!"

When the crisis is over, you need to calm down. That's when the boss's second worker steps in: the parasympathetic nervous system. It puts things back to normal so you can rest and digest.

Trigger Happy

Imagine you're a police officer chasing a murder suspect down a dark alley. Your radio crackles. "Armed and dangerous," you hear. Still running, you draw your gun and put your finger on the trigger.

Suddenly, a dog barks at you from a balcony.

Bang!

Nearby, a window shatters. Someone screams.

The suspect disappears, and you're left stunned. What happened?

When that dog barked, it startled you. Automatically, you crouched, you blinked, you clenched your hands. And when your hands clenched, your gun fired — long before your conscious mind decided how to respond.

That's what might have happened to real police officers a couple of decades ago, before scientists started wondering how guns and the startle response work together. (The answer: not well.)

In 2003, a professor named Roger Enoka at the University of Colorado wrote a paper about involuntary muscle contractions — a fancy way of saying "moving by accident." Roger and his students found three things that could make a police officer fire accidentally:

The startle response. Think of the barking dog.

A balance disturbance. An officer slips on a banana peel and fires her gun.

Limb interaction. The left hand wrestles the suspect to the ground. The right hand wants in on the action.

A few years and a few accidental shootings later, researchers in Germany did another set of experiments. They put pressure sensors on a gun, then asked police

Built Like a Beetle

Creatures big and small show the fight-or-flight response. At the University of Georgia, researchers tested a type of super-strong horned beetle. The bugs lifted one hundred times their own weight. Then the researchers added stress by tapping the beetles' shells to scare them. Under pressure, the average beetle lifted three hundred times its own weight. That's like a little kid lifting a dumpster!

officers to hold the device in one hand while doing complicated stuff with the other. About one-fifth of the officers accidentally hit the trigger, and a few hit it with enough force to make the gun fire.

For police departments, there were only two choices: remove the world's dogs, or change the way officers held their guns. Today, officers might still draw their weapons while they chase down suspects. But until they're in immediate danger, they keep their fingers *off* the trigger.

Flying Off the Handle

On May 31, 2009, Air France Flight 447 took off from Rio de Janeiro, Brazil, bound for Paris. The air turned cold and turbulent along the way, and ice crystals formed on the plane's speed probes. With the instruments out of commission, the crew made some adjustments to the course and flight speed. Nothing seemed too serious ...

Until the engines died.

A mechanical voice repeated "stall" over and over again. Warnings beeped. Crew members yelled desperately to one another as the plane fell. During a stall, pilots are supposed to nose the aircraft down to recover. But the off-kilter instruments said the plane was already too low, so the panicked pilots pushed the nose higher instead.

Less than four minutes after the stall, the plane hit the Atlantic Ocean, killing everyone on board.

A few years later, researchers in Australia gathered data from this crash, along with information from other crashes caused by sudden crises. They found that surprised and scared airline pilots might be hampered by their own fight-or-flight reflexes. With hearts racing and focus narrowed, pilots reacted with too much adrenaline and not enough analysis. If the pilots on the Air France flight had realized the instruments were wrong, for example, they would have made vastly different decisions.

The Australian researchers made recommendations for pilot training — suggestions that are now used by airlines all over the world. Instead of practicing for specific emergencies, today's pilots-in-training are surprised by buzzers and alarms, unexpected catastrophes and sudden drops. The more they train, the better — and safer — the decisions they make under pressure.

Over the past decade, studies on police officers, soldiers and pilots have all shown the same thing: people can successfully "practice" being surprised. With experience, our brains handle shock better and bounce back to work more quickly.

Code Red-ish

The doors of the hospital emergency room whoosh open and a woman staggers inside, clutching her chest. She's shaking and sweating. Her heart's racing, she's flushed and she can't breathe.

Nurses whisk her onto a gurney. Soon, she's attached to an electrocardiogram (EKG) machine that monitors the electrical activity of her heart. But the readings look fine, and so do the results of her blood tests.

What's going on?

Like thousands of other people who rush to emergency rooms each year, the woman has not suffered from a heart attack, but from a panic attack. She's been gripped by intense fear. Her nervous system has switched to full

fight-or-flight mode, and stress hormones are racing through her system. Her muscles have constricted and her mind is on red alert, ready to battle an enemy that doesn't exist.

Panic attacks are like fight-or-flight misfires, and researchers haven't figured out exactly why they occur. They can happen when someone is worried about a future event or having trouble dealing with past trauma. Or they can stem from a physical condition, such as a thyroid disorder.

Panic attacks happen most often to people who endure long-term stress, people with phobias and people going through life crises. They're more common in women (though women are also more likely to be misdiagnosed with a panic attack when they're actually having a heart attack).

Fortunately, these attacks don't last long. The average panic attack peaks within ten minutes and ends within half an hour. And for people who suffer repeated attacks, there are therapies and medications that can help.

In the 1960s, a psychologist at the University of Waterloo and a professor at the University of Massachusetts had a conversation that went something like this:

> **Walter Fenz:** How can we study people who are really stressed out?
>
> **Seymour Epstein:** Oooh, I know! Let's throw them from a plane.

They gathered groups of skydivers and studied their stress levels before and during a big jump. Here's what they found:

The people who were skydiving for the first time were looking forward to the jump and were relaxed in the hours leading up to it. But moments before the plane doors opened, those first-time jumpers were seriously stressed! One of them couldn't keep his knees from knocking together. Another missed his jump because he couldn't figure out whether to step forward with his left foot or his right. Under pressure, their brains and their bodies did all sorts of unusual things.

The instructors, people who had jumped hundreds of times before, were fairly calm when the plane doors opened. They'd learned to cope with that pressure. But strangely, they felt stress in the hours *before* takeoff, worrying about all the things that might go wrong.

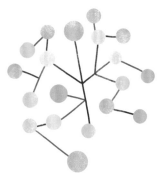

Through experiments like this one, researchers identified two kinds of stress. There's the fight-or-flight response we feel in a crisis, and there's the simmering stress caused by worry. They also pinpointed some key causes of stress, which are just plain "N.U.T.S.":

Novelty: New experiences can be scary.
Unpredictability: The teacher mentions a pop quiz.
Threat to the Ego: When a bully looms or a parent criticizes, our self-confidence dips and we get anxious.
Sense of Control: You feel the plane going down, and you can't do anything to stop it!

Each type of stressful situation prompts the body to release hormones and chemicals. And if those chemicals float around in our bodies often enough, or for long enough, they can damage our health. That's why doctors and scientists and even military officials have spent years and years studying the science of stress.

Stress Busters

Your fight-or-flight response isn't always something to overcome. It's part of your survival instinct. But if you're planning a professional tightroping career or a knife-juggling tour, here are a few ways to keep your brain in balance:

Breathe. People can breathe automatically *or* on purpose. Many researchers believe that by consciously controlling our breath, we are sending signals to our brains and saying, "Hey, everything's okay."

Act. It doesn't really matter what you choose to do. If you can overcome your startle response by taking action, you'll get your brain back to work more quickly.

Practice. We react automatically to sudden stimuli. When we hear a strange noise, we jump. But our brains also learn. By exposing ourselves to that strange noise over and over again, we can teach ourselves there's nothing to fear. Practice is like a vaccine for the brain.

Chapter 2

The Long Game

Welcome to the fair! Step right up for your free ticket.

Do you love roller coasters? Maybe you scream through every loop-the-loop but emerge with a giant smile on your face? Well, do we have a deal for you. Today's special is a permanent coaster ride. You get to spend all day, every day, on the track.

Wait ... what?

That sounds terrible. No one — not even the most committed adrenaline junkie — would take that deal.

But some of us *do* put our bodies through constant roller-coaster stress. And while one ride can be a rush, ongoing stress causes all sorts of health problems. Remember Hans Selye, the guy from Chapter 1 who first defined stress? He noticed that animals exposed to constant tension had heart attacks, kidney issues and strokes. Since then, scientists have linked long-term pressure to other health problems, too.

Our stress responses evolved to help us deal with major crises, such as lions and bears, earthquakes and tornadoes, forest fires and landslides. Those are all things humans can fight or flee. But we're not so well equipped for the ongoing pressures of modern life. In a single day, you might have a fight with a frenemy, a math test and an after-school dentist appointment. Even though these stressors aren't emergencies, they trigger powerful fight-or-flight hormones.

No one wants a constant adrenaline rush. No one wants to feel permanently anxious or depressed. So why can't we all calm down?

Five-Alarm Lives

Soldier, firefighter, paramedic, police officer. Those are the four most stressful jobs in the world according to *Forbes* magazine. And that means military personnel and first responders might face a higher risk of these issues:

Heart disease. When people are stressed, their blood pressure rises and their blood grows thicker — ready to clot in case of an injury. This can lead to serious heart issues over time.

Immune system breakdowns. The stress hormone cortisol also regulates inflammation in the body. If too much cortisol is released too often, immune cells stop responding. They can't regulate inflammation as well. That leaves the body vulnerable to bacteria, viruses and even cancer.

Mental illness. A constant overdose of stress hormones messes with brain chemistry. People feel on edge and anxious. Or they miss out on their necessary feel-good signals and end up with depression.

Addiction. Substances such as alcohol and tobacco release chemicals in the brain that can help people feel better — temporarily. Relying on this short-term solution can lead to addiction, with terrible mental and physical side effects.

Eating Disorders. Doctors are just beginning to study the way stress and eating interact.

Reading that list is probably enough to send any stress-case straight to the doctor. And we *could* all cross "soldier" and "firefighter" off our list of career goals. Would that do the trick?

Apparently not.

The traumas of war and migration leave refugee children at higher risk for stress-related illnesses. In Turkey, therapists bridge language barriers by using art therapy to help kids of Syrian refugees share their experiences and learn coping strategies.

In 2015, Ontario's Centre for Addiction and Mental Health surveyed more than ten thousand high school students. A third of those kids reported "psychological distress" — problems with home life, school, health or addiction.

The researchers were shocked — that was a 10 percent increase over their findings from just two years before. More kids rated their mental health as "fair" or "poor." More had visited mental health professionals, and twice as many were on medication for anxiety or depression.

Could kids really be getting more and more stressed?

Studies from other parts of the world have shown similar findings. A survey by the American Psychological Association found that one-third of teens felt overwhelmed or depressed because of pressure. In countries where college entrance exams can make or break someone's future, stress levels soar even higher.

In one study, scientists compared students in Korea and America who were hoping to attend university. The Korean students spent little time on leisure and almost half their time on homework (twice the number of study hours American students spent). They felt more negative about their study hours than the Americans did, and 36 percent of them were clinically depressed. Only 16 percent of the American students showed similar

symptoms. But in both countries, more homework and more negative feelings about homework meant a higher rate of depression.

Obviously, it's not only soldiers and police officers who face long-term stress. Kids feel it, too. And that's a major problem, because stress has serious effects on the developing brain. Over time, our neural connections can short-circuit. The amygdalae — those "reptilian" centers responsible for our instincts — start sensing danger where no real threat exists.

Studies show that stressed-out kids have memory problems, are more easily confused and often have trouble forming friendships. Sometimes, kids under pressure get more aggressive because their brains are stuck in fight-or-flight mode.

So what's the stress solution? Researchers, doctors and counselors point to two main steps:

Protect kids from stress overload, especially when they're young. That means parents and schools working together to make sure schedules are reasonable and students aren't crushed under a mountain of activities and homework.

Teach students to recognize and deal with pressure. From breathing techniques to sleep schedules, and meditation to medication, there are plenty of options for all ages and all anxiety levels.

The good news is there's change in progress. For example, many schools are starting to teach mindfulness techniques, even to primary students. (More on that in Chapter 5.) But what about the people who need to perform under intense stress? What about the people who can't stop to meditate? Sometimes, we need the pressure players to step up to the plate.

Catch and Release

How is stress like the common cold? It's contagious! Researchers at the University of British Columbia tested cortisol levels in the saliva of four hundred elementary school kids. They figured out which classrooms had more stressed-out kids. Then they compared those results to stress-tested teachers.

Classrooms with stressed kids had unhappy teachers, and vice versa. But which came first? Tired teachers who let their classrooms run wild might have caused stressed-out students. Or kids with anxiety and behavior problems might have led to burnt-out teachers. Researchers are planning more studies ... and they might find both are true.

Outbreak!

Carlo Urbani was a big-shot doctor. For years, he'd worked with Médecins Sans Frontières (also known as Doctors Without Borders), a nonprofit organization that offers medical care in developing countries and war zones. He and a team of his colleagues accepted a Nobel Prize for their efforts in 1999.

Four years later, the Italian-born doctor had transferred his talents to the World Health Organization (WHO). He was in Hanoi, Vietnam, working to fight malaria, when local doctors called him for advice. They had a Chinese American business executive in the hospital with the flu. But his flu wasn't getting better, and the doctors and nurses were also getting

sick. They had fevers, coughs and difficulty breathing.

Immediately, Carlo put the original patient and the sick medical staff into isolation. Then he and a team of researchers began taking samples. Within a week, Carlo knew they weren't battling the flu. This was something new.

He sounded the alarm. WHO launched the biggest response ever. It flew in disease specialists and warned the world of the threat. It tracked the virus to an outbreak in China.

The disease became known as severe acute respiratory syndrome (SARS). Carlo and his colleagues worked to contain and treat patients as quickly as possible. But even with their efforts, more than seven hundred people in thirty-seven countries died before the disease was brought under control.

Carlo himself was infected. As he lay in the hospital, his wife was only allowed to speak to him through an intercom. She was devastated. Why had he exposed himself to so many sick people? Here's what Carlo answered: "If I cannot even work in such situations, what am I here for? Answering emails, going to cocktail parties and pushing paper?" Carlo died on March 29, 2003, still committed to his work.

"Every man that undertakes to bee of a profession or takes upon himself an office must take all parts of it, the good and the evill, the pleasure and the pain ..." That's what English doctor William Boghurst wrote in 1665 when he chose to stay in London and treat bubonic plague victims.

 Hospital Heroics

Since the SARS outbreak, researchers have studied people like Carlo. That's because in the face of major epidemics, doctors and nurses experience days and weeks of high-level stress. They toil around the clock, risking their own health.

As a society, we *need* these medical professionals to keep working. Hopefully, they won't have to sacrifice their lives, but we do want them to endure under stress.

Some doctors and nurses stay on duty because they know they're the only ones with the skills and expertise

to help in dire situations. Others stay because of religious or ethical beliefs. Often, they persevere even when their own families are at risk. When Hurricane Katrina struck New Orleans in 2005, almost all emergency room doctors kept working for at least the first five days.

Doctors in these sorts of situations face tremendous amounts of pressure. So what can we do, as a society, to keep their stress levels under control?

Researchers have made two big suggestions:

While the doctors care for patients, we need to care for the doctors. They should have the best safety equipment; emergency responders should check on their families; and we should provide mental health support for them after a crisis.

Doctors need good information. They shouldn't be choosing whether to stay at work based on rumors — they might make terrible decisions! They need to know if conditions are getting worse and what's being done to help. They can then use that information to make the best choices for themselves and their patients.

Recently, scientists have started taking a closer look at these high-pressure situations, trying to figure out exactly how emergencies affect real-life decision-making. The ways doctors function under stress might help us all find better ways to manage.

Brain Games

Have you ever felt so busy that you "can't think straight"? It's not just a phrase. People under pressure are less likely to use logic and more likely to rely on instinct or snap judgments. They give more weight to the best-case scenario, instead of considering what might go wrong.

Some studies suggest that men are likely to make risky choices when they're stressed, while women spend too much time worrying. Here's a simple scenario: Imagine a group of people on a sinking ship. There's a life raft nearby, but a much fancier lifeboat a huge leap away. A greater percentage of men might risk the unsafe leap. A higher number of women might continue weighing their options while the ship sinks beneath them.

All of this is why emergency responders don't rely on instinct. Instead, they memorize the actions they should take in a crisis. Firefighters, for example, might need to sound an alarm, evacuate the area and rescue people who are stranded before helping people who've been hurt. It wouldn't make sense to help one wounded person while leaving a dozen others inside a burning building. Having a preset order helps ensure the firefighters make the best decisions, even in the midst of flames and alarms.

Soldiers, police officers, paramedics and emergency room doctors follow similar steps. When the 2015 earthquake in Nepal triggered an avalanche at Everest Base Camp, Rachel Tullet was buried under a layer of ice. But the New Zealand doctor was trained in emergency medicine. Once she dug herself out, she surveyed the situation and calmly began sorting patients. Some she treated on-site, others she sent down the mountain for help and others she certified as dead. She did all of this with a cracked kneecap and a leg wound — a wound that she later stitched herself, without anesthetic.

Her fellow climbers credited Rachel with saving twenty-three lives — something she never could have accomplished if she'd panicked when the avalanche struck.

What does all of this mean for regular people? Research suggests that if we're too stressed to think straight, we should probably slow down and think twice.

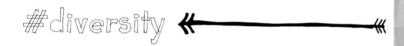

#diversity

Pop quiz: When did America's National Institutes of Health tell scientists they had to use male *and* female test subjects in their research? Was it back in 1920, when women won the right to vote?

Nope. It wasn't until 2016.

For decades, researchers used only male subjects in their stress experiments. They figured males had fewer monthly hormone changes to interfere with the results. It turns out that (a) those scientists were just plain wrong — menstrual cycles don't affect results — and (b) there are important gender differences when it comes to stress.

A New York researcher named Georgia E. Hodes studied both male and female rats and found that while it took three weeks of chronic stress to cause anxiety and depression in male rats, it took only six days to produce the same reactions in females. Georgia suggested the difference might be related to a tiny region of the brain called the nucleus accumbens. The female rats had a more active gene there that stopped pleasure messages at the gate. *Sorry, we're stressed here!*

Locomotion

Mateusz Szymanski was driving a commuter train through western Poland in 2016 when he spotted a truck on the tracks. Immediately, Mateusz pulled the emergency break to slow the carriages. But he knew they wouldn't stop in time. He raced back through the rows of seats, yelling at people to brace themselves. The passengers threw themselves to the floor, and the driver made a last-minute grab for a safety bar before the train hit the truck, tearing metal and spraying shards of glass. No one was hurt — thanks mainly to the actions of Mateusz. Under pressure, he did everything right.

No time for good news! When that gene was removed, the female rats acted more like the males.

Other studies suggest that in a crisis, females stay alert for longer. That might be a useful survival trait. (There's a reason no one wants to get between a mama bear and her cubs.) But under chronic stress, those survival instincts keep churning for too long. They can cause problems with sleep, digestion, attention span and anxiety. Trying to make calm, logical decisions while you're stressed is like trying to read a book while your hyperactive little brother jumps up and down on the couch demanding attention!

There's a lot more research to be done. Right now, scientists are mainly sure of one thing: differences in hormones, genes and brain pathways mean that men and women deal with stress differently.

Of course, rats and people may handle it differently, too.

In crises, some people achieve heroic feats. Others crumble. Scientists say there are two main reasons for the differences:

Our genes. Slight variations in hormone production and nerve receptors can have a major impact on how you respond to sudden danger. If you jump at the tiniest sound and quiver through Disney movies, blame your ancestors!

Our past. People who've suffered abuse or lived through trauma can find it more difficult to manage stress. On the other hand, people trained to react quickly and calmly do better in emergency situations.

The good news (and the bad)? On a scale from supercool to cry-and-crumble, most of us are somewhere in between.

Stress Busters

There are many great ways to manage stress. You can check out Chapter 5 for all the latest research. In the meantime, here are some of the best strategies for riding the roller coaster of everyday life:

Sleep. Take away all the screens from your room, head to bed at the same time each night and aim for nine hours of sleep if you're a teen.

Exercise. The American Psychological Association calls exercise a "small but powerful change." Even a brisk walk can help your body and brain produce the feel-good chemicals that reduce anxiety and depression.

Ask for help. Psychologists and counselors have tools and tricks to combat stress. If you find that anxiety or depression is changing your everyday life, talk to your parents or a trusted adult. It might be time to see your doctor and ask for a referral.

Chapter 3

Bounce Back

A bubble bath, cocoa with marshmallows, a hug from Mom or Dad, a venting session with friends, a hike in the woods: these are all ways we deal with stress. But there are some problems that can't be solved by hot chocolate or a heart-to-heart.

In the past few decades, scientists have learned more about trauma and how it affects the human brain. Sometimes, a single event — a car accident, for example, or a brush with death — can cause lasting emotional turmoil. Other people are scarred by repeated abuse or the prolonged violence of war. Some experiences are so overwhelming, they continue to disturb people for months, or even years.

But not everyone who faces trauma ends up with lasting symptoms. Sometimes, disaster victims recover more quickly than expected. A few even turn their experiences into positive change. So while scientists study possible causes and treatments for stress-induced illnesses, they also explore something else: resilience.

If we can understand how some people bounce back, we can help others do the same.

War-Torn

In 1994, twelve-year-old Norman Okello was kidnapped. He was snatched by soldiers of the Lord's Resistance Army (LRA), a rebel group battling for control of Uganda in East Africa. Norman was beaten again and again before he was inducted into a battalion. He was then forced to kill another soldier to prove his loyalty.

Soon, Norman was a full-fledged fighter. He took specialized artillery training, raided enemy army camps and tortured captives. Each day brought new violence.

Aid groups estimate that up to 38 000 children like Norman were kidnapped by the LRA before the United States intervened to help the Ugandan government in 2011. Thousands of child soldiers died; those who survived faced a difficult road. It wasn't easy to forget the war zone and head back to school to learn the rules of grammar or the even more complicated rules of everyday friendship.

That's exactly what Norman discovered when he escaped after two years with the rebel army. His life didn't return to normal. He had so many nightmares, he was scared to fall asleep at night. He flew into sudden rages and picked fights with other teens. He couldn't manage the demands of day-to-day life, and he didn't understand why. But, as Norman would discover, he was part of a long line of soldiers who suffered strange aftereffects of war …

War Wounds

Hot off the press: the *Diagnostic and Statistical Manual of Mental Disorders*!

Does it sound like an instant bestseller? Maybe not, but doctors and psychologists rely every day on the book they call the *DSM*. It's an important catalog of mental illnesses and conditions.

In 1980, the *DSM* listed a condition called post-traumatic stress disorder (PTSD) for the first time. By including it, the book gave an official name to a list of symptoms that had haunted people and confused doctors for centuries.

In the 1800s, some of the men who returned home from the American Civil War were diagnosed with a condition called "soldier's heart." They suffered from heart palpitations, sudden pains, disturbed sleep and digestive problems. No one could figure out why. Was it physical or mental? Had they eaten something wrong, endured the cold for too long, weathered too many diseases? Or had they simply lost their minds?

During World War I, the condition resurfaced with a new name. When doctors saw soldiers who had nightmares, tremors or heart palpitations, they diagnosed "shell shock." They thought that days and nights of enemy bombing had rattled soldiers' brains. But the army desperately needed soldiers, so men with shell shock were often sent straight back into battle — with disastrous results. The British army alone executed 150 shell-shocked soldiers for "displaying cowardice" when their damaged minds and bodies turned away from the fighting.

During World War II, shell shock was renamed "battle fatigue," and doctors finally recognized it as a psychiatric condition. They started offering psychiatric services on the front lines, hoping to keep as many soldiers as possible in the fight. It wasn't a perfect solution, but it *was* better than execution.

Finally, after Vietnam War veterans in the United States campaigned for better care, the world began to recognize post-traumatic stress disorder. It's a condition often linked with soldiers, especially after more than one-fifth of veterans who served in Iraq and Afghanistan showed symptoms. But PTSD isn't always the result of war. It can affect victims of child abuse, car accidents and earthquakes. It can appear in senior citizens or in children.

People suffering from PTSD don't always see a memory as a story, the way the rest of us do. Instead, they experience intense emotion, often triggered by a recognized sound, smell or sight. The logical brain shuts down, fear wells up and fight-or-flight responses take over.

PTSD is what made it so hard for child soldier Norman Okello to attend school or play with other kids. He'd endured years of violence, and he couldn't leave those experiences behind. Often, he found himself shaking with rage. Then, ten years after his escape, Norman found help at the offices of a foreign-aid organization. By meeting with psychologists, bonding with other former child soldiers and sharing his story, he began to deal with his anger.

Eventually, Norman was able to marry and start a family of his own.

Common Ground

During World War II, the Japanese government celebrated the country's unbreakable national spirit — *yamato damashii*. This strong cultural belief was rigidly upheld — especially in the military. Stress disorders among soldiers were hidden because they contradicted the idea that Japanese fighters were mentally invincible.

Fortunately for today's historians and researchers, a few army psychiatrists broke the rules and preserved their patient records. That's how we know that soldiers in Japan suffered the same trauma symptoms as soldiers in other parts of the world.

People who suffer from PTSD have smaller hippocampi. But doctors don't know which comes first. Do people get PTSD because those areas of the brain are smaller, or do the hippocampi shrink because of PTSD? There's still more research to be done ...

Here are some things doctors look for when diagnosing PTSD:

- recurring memories and flashbacks
- nightmares
- avoidance of trauma-related triggers
- depression, loneliness or extreme moodiness
- aggressive or reckless behavior
- trouble concentrating

Some people who suffer from PTSD feel as if they're outside their own bodies, watching a stranger muddle through stressful situations. Doctors call this "dissociation."

Over the past few decades, researchers have found physical changes that might contribute to PTSD. They believe that trauma damages the hippocampi, two seahorse-shaped areas in the middle of the brain. Usually, our hippocampi help with memory and navigation; they also serve as decision-making centers in conflict situations. When damaged, they can lead us astray.

Other parts of our brain can also change. Under stress, the prefrontal cortex learns to prompt certain reactions. It might tell you to drop to the ground at the sound of gunfire, for example. Scientists think that some brains have trouble "unlearning" these responses. If you repeatedly duck and cover during battle, then you might return home and drop to the ground every time there's a loud noise.

A third possible PTSD culprit: cortisol. It's one of the stress hormones we learned about in Chapter I. But strangely, people with PTSD have *lower* cortisol levels. And because one of cortisol's jobs is to balance adrenaline, less cortisol can mean more anxiety. (This isn't something people can control; cortisol levels are probably genetic.)

People with PTSD have trouble scanning their environments for the cues — children laughing, birds singing, music playing — that tell us we're safe. Their brains can't decide whether ringing phones or car horns are dangerous. The world becomes a bombardment of overlapping signals.

Fortunately, doctors and researchers have found many ways to help victims of trauma. For some, they prescribe medication. They send others to counseling, where patients learn to retrain their brains. Often, they do both.

PTSD sufferers also find relief through meditation or yoga. They might express themselves through art therapy, or meet in support groups, online or in person. Doctors sometimes suggest people take classes to help them face their fears. For example, a person who was attacked might find empowerment through martial arts lessons.

Poetic License

"In thy faint slumbers I by thee have watched, and heard thee murmur tales of iron wars ..." In Shakespeare's *Henry IV*, Lady Percy worries about her husband, a former soldier. She says he can't sleep, he's depressed and he startles easily. It seems Shakespeare understood the symptoms of PTSD four centuries before the *DSM*.

Researchers are also experimenting with high-tech solutions, such as brain-computer interaction devices. A technician attaches electrodes to a patient's scalp to read the brain waves. A computer screen then gives positive feedback (more colors or faster spaceships) when the patient calms his or her brain activity. Over time, this helps retrain the nerve connections inside the brain. Patients who practice often have significantly fewer PTSD symptoms.

Of course, high tech isn't the only route to healing. Lately, a few programs have matched PTSD sufferers with new and helpful friends — of an unexpected sort.

The Canine Cure

Dogs aren't the only therapy animals. Children who survived the 2013 tornadoes in Oklahoma later bonded with specially trained miniature horses.

As he headed to work in 1996, California social worker Rick Yount whistled for Gabe, his golden retriever. He had a hunch the dog might be helpful, and he was right. That day, as Rick drove a small eleven-year-old boy to a new foster home, Gabe offered both distraction and comfort. He made the tough trip a tiny bit easier.

By 2008, Gabe was an officially certified therapy dog. He'd worked with all sorts of people. So when soldiers began returning from Iraq and Afghanistan, some with physical and mental injuries, Rick had a unique idea. What if he asked soldiers with PTSD to help train assistance dogs? Once trained, the dogs could help veterans with physical disabilities.

His program was a huge success. A year later, Rick was invited to work at Walter Reed Army Medical Center in Washington, D.C. There, in 2011, he helped found the Warrior Canine Connection.

By training new assistance dogs, veterans with PTSD

improve their physical health, find themselves rejoining their communities (at the dog park, for example) and learn job skills for the future. The veterans say they feel calmer, happier and safer after working with the animals.

Along with a team of researchers, Rick has shown that training assistance dogs might increase levels of oxytocin in the brains of veterans. Oxytocin is sometimes called "the love hormone." It helps people form relationships, it reduces fear and it promotes trust. When given to veterans in pill form, it can decrease the symptoms of PTSD. In canine form, it may prove even more powerful.

Are they superstrong? Genetically different? Or just plain lucky?

Most people who experience a traumatic event, such as a car accident, recover on their own, without needing years of treatment and support. Scientists want to know how they do it.

Genetics probably help. On page 34, we explored the physical differences between the brains of people with PTSD and the brains of people without. Our DNA might hold other secrets, too.

Genes are kind of like light switches — they can be turned on or turned off. The study of those on/off switches is called epigenetics. New research suggests that when people endure trauma, certain genes are turned on, or expressed. When those people have children, the expressed genes can be passed to the next generation. That means if a woman survives a terrorist attack, her future kids might be at greater risk for PTSD.

The world around us also makes a difference to our resilience. Harvard researcher Theresa Betancourt spent years working with children affected by war and trauma in Rwanda.

She found the most resilient kids had three things:

* trust in other people
* strong community support
* self-confidence and courage

In Rwanda, that courage is called *kwigirira ikizere*: "a strong heart."

It's not often that researchers try to measure love, but that seems to be the thing that helps most. Resilient kids (and grown-ups) have loving families and friends. Other research has shown they often have strong spiritual beliefs and faith that the future will be brighter.

Fight, Flight or Friendship

Psychology professor Shelley Taylor had a few key questions for stress researchers.

Shelley: Who did you test for fight-or-flight responses?
Scientists: Men
Shelley: Who did you test for cortisol levels?
Scientists: Men
Shelley: Who decided to run these tests only on men?
Scientists: Men

Along with a team of researchers in California, Shelley set out to research stress in both men *and* women. Eventually, she suggested that fight-or-flight wasn't the only possible response to danger. There was another common reaction, especially in women.

In 2000, after reviewing decades of research, her group called their theory "tend and befriend." In times of danger, instead of fighting or fleeing, some people care for, or "tend," those around them. Tending to children actually increases levels of oxytocin (the love hormone) in women's bodies, which in turn lowers stress hormones.

In dangerous situations, people also "befriend." They gather in groups, the same way ducks might form a tight circle on a pond when predators are near. For humans, just as for ducks, there's often safety in numbers.

Some of the most interesting tend-and-befriend research examines stressful situations that no one could fight or flee: earthquakes. After the Wenchuan earthquake in China in 2008, scientists interviewed more than two thousand women — most of whom were undereducated, poor and living in tents or temporary shelters. Many suffered from symptoms of PTSD. But those surrounded by strong social

networks had the least severe symptoms. The researchers found that by bonding with others, women decreased their own stress responses, improved their quality of life and enhanced quality of life for those around them.

In 2014, a year after a devastating earthquake in Turkey, researchers tested and interviewed more than a thousand women there. The earthquake had disrupted many people's marriages, families and friendships. Still, those with the strongest neighborhood support networks were most protected from the negative effects of trauma.

There's much more research to be done into the ways hormones and brain pathways affect stress responses, and how our bodies and brains choose between fight-or-flight and tend-and-befriend. But after traumatic events, it seems that friendship is sometimes the best route to recovery.

"Post-traumatic growth." Is that a strange kind of wart on your big toe?

Nope.

It's the scientific name for "giving your head a shake."

Imagine you're lounging by the pool when your cruise ship strikes an undersea reef. People all around you panic, but you stay calm. You help direct people into lifeboats, you rescue a child from the waves and then you swim to safety. Afterward, as you replay the events in your mind, you think:

- I'm so thankful I survived!
- Hey, I did pretty well back there. I'm stronger than I thought.
- What was I doing wasting my life on the sundeck? I should join the coast guard!

After a major earthquake shook Chile in 2010, researchers interviewed survivors about the changes in their lives. They found lots of people who felt more spiritually connected, more capable and confident and more interested in new challenges and ideas.

Scientists in Los Angeles had similar findings when they interviewed young cancer survivors. One of them said: "Cancer has given my life a different perspective. In a way, cancer gave me a gift. A gift the average person cannot comprehend. I saw the best in human nature when I was sick."

At first glance, post-traumatic growth might seem like the opposite of PTSD. But here's the good news: even people who suffer extreme aftereffects of stress can go on to drastically improve their lives. It's possible to have trauma *and* growth.

Stress Busters

You don't have to be a returning soldier to suffer from stress. People who have experienced abuse, witnessed an accident or had a brush with death might find themselves in need of support. If you or someone you know has symptoms of PTSD, here's where to start:

Seek help. Doctors and counselors know more about PTSD than ever before. There are many types of treatment for all kinds of people, so talk to your school counselor or your family doctor and ask about your options.

Explore resources. Both the National Center for PTSD in the United States and the PTSD Association of Canada help people who are suffering from trauma-related stress.

Build a strong support network. People who recover best are those surrounded by family and friends. So share your experiences, join a support group, take your dog to the park or volunteer at the seniors' home down the street.

As you heal, explore new interests. Some people manage to use traumatic events to kick-start their dreams.

Chapter 4

Helpful Highs

You're at a school dance, waving your arms in the air while the bass thumps and the lights swirl. Then, suddenly, your friends push you up on stage. They shove a microphone in your hands. The crowd starts chanting, "Sing! Sing! Sing!"

Yikes! You can't even carry a tune. What should you do?

A. Run crying from the gym.
B. Take a deep breath and tell yourself to calm down.
C. Holler out your best off-key karaoke song and end with a mic drop.

Your fight-or-flight response would choose Option A. Your common sense might suggest you keep calm. But researchers would recommend Option C. "Get excited" is sometimes better advice than "calm down." By thinking of your stress as something positive — the way you might view an adrenaline rush — you can improve your performance.

This chapter's all about the upsides of stress, from the high of intense competition to the endorphin rush of success. Stress can drive you to accomplish more than you think. It might even help you carry a tune.

Pumped Up

Alison Wood Brooks wasn't a stress researcher; she was a business professor at Harvard University. But as she studied and trained busy executives, Alison noticed that smart, capable people were often limited by anxiety. Before a big presentation, they'd have sweaty palms. They'd forget things. They'd doubt their abilities.

Alison wondered if a tiny adjustment in perception might help people deal with their butterflies. She set up three separate experiments. In the first, she asked participants to sing in front of a stranger. In the second, she made a group prepare speeches and then record themselves on camera. For the third group, she created a difficult math exam.

Alison asked half the participants of each group to prepare by repeating, "I'm calm. I'm calm." She told the other half to repeat, "I'm excited! I'm excited!" Those statements — calm or excited — were the only differences between the groups.

Power Play

Repeating the phrase "I'm excited" is an example of something called a "mindset intervention."

Want to try one yourself?

Before your next test, spend two minutes acting like the most powerful person in the world. Stand with a swagger. Put your hands on your hips. Make your body open and expansive. You might improve your mark!

Scientists at Columbia and Harvard universities showed that by holding power poses for two minutes, people could increase testosterone and decrease cortisol in their bodies. Those changes meant more confidence and less stress.

The effects were obvious. In all three experiments, the excited group did significantly better. The singers felt more confident and hit the right notes more often. The public speakers were more persuasive, competent and persistent. The test-takers felt better about their math skills and scored higher on the exam.

How could such a big change come from switching one sentence?

Alison and her team suggest we can't easily calm down when we feel stress. After all, the reaction is biological. We can't cancel a chemical process in our bodies. But if we change the way we *think* about stress — view it as anticipation instead of anxiety — we can change the way we perform.

That's something athletes and coaches recognized long before scientists.

Nerves of ... Pudding?

As Greek track star Alexi Pappas prepared to race at the 2016 Olympics, she didn't worry about getting the jitters. Alexi told a reporter from the *New York Times* that even nightmares didn't bother her. Before past events, she'd dreamed she was running in clown shoes or struggling to race through pudding. To Alexi, these dreams were simply signs that she cared deeply about her sport.

"Nervous is a cousin to excited," she said.

When we face an intense situation, we feel the fight-or-flight response within our bodies. Our hands quiver; our hearts race. But we can't necessarily tell if those things are happening because of danger or excitement. Remember the surprise party and the lion attack in Chapter 1? Even though one is good and

the other is bad, both prompt similar physical responses.

Scientists call this the difference between a "challenge state" and a "threat state."

A track star like Alexi has control over the decision to enter a tough race. She feels confident she can perform well, and she sees the event as one step toward her goal of a track career. Those three things — control, confidence and goal-setting — help her see a race as a challenge, not a threat. That means when the starting gun sounds, she'll get a useful burst of adrenaline and an automatic heart-rate increase.

What she won't get? An extra serving of stress hormones. If Alexi saw the race as a threat, her body would respond with more cortisol. That could make focus and movement harder. In golfers, baseball players and cricketers, researchers have shown that challenge states boost performance, while threat states make everything more difficult.

Lost your math homework? As you're rummaging through your room, try to think of the hunt as a challenge. Scientists have shown that our visual search abilities are better when we're challenged and worse when we feel threatened.

Eighty-one men and nineteen women lined up on the New River Gorge Bridge in West Virginia, each equipped with a lightweight parachute. They were there for Bridge Day 2014, the biggest legal BASE jumping event in the United States. Each was about to leap from the steel span and free fall toward the rapids 267 m (876 ft.) below. With luck, they'd plummet for two to six seconds, deploy their mini-parachutes and then land in what looked like a postage stamp — a tiny patch of parking lot on the far side of the river.

BASE jumping is the most dangerous of extreme sports. The name "BASE" stands for Building, Antenna, Span and Earth: the things from which a participant might leap. None of those jumps is safe; for every sixty sport participants, one will eventually die.

On the bridge across the New River Gorge in 2014, the one hundred jumpers did something a little unusual. They each spit into a vial to help scientists measure their stress levels. Researchers had already given the athletes a string of personality tests. Now, by measuring stress hormones in the saliva samples, they'd be able to figure out whether BASE jumpers felt stress like the rest of us.

The answer: sort of.

Beginner jumpers felt the most stressed; expert jumpers felt the least. But all the athletes showed a fairly normal stress response. There was one major difference between BASE jumpers and regular, everyday folk. On the personality tests, many jumpers showed low "harm avoidance." They assess risks differently than the rest of us.

BASE jumper: Let's jump off a cliff.
Friend: That's crazy, dude. We could die!
BASE jumper: Nah, we'll be fine.

Another study showed that jumpers continued to trust in their own safety even after witnessing disasters. Three-quarters had seen another jumper die or get seriously injured. Three-quarters had also experienced a brush with death. And yet they all continued to look down from bridges and assume they'd be okay.

That's taking the challenge state to a whole new level.

Go with the Flow

Have you ever felt "in the zone"? So absorbed by an activity that you no longer notice time passing?

Researchers call this a "flow state," and it happens to all sorts of people: athletes, artists, even chess players. Scientists who studied sixty-three chess competitors found that when players were overwhelmed, their stress hormones rose too high to be helpful. But players who hit just the right kind of match — not too easy, not too hard — showed moderate levels of cortisol and great focus in their games. They were "in the zone."

This isn't a new discovery. In 1908, two American psychologists named Robert M. Yerkes and John Dillingham Dodson showed a relationship between excitement and performance. Both went up ... for a while. But if excitement levels went *too* high, then performance decreased. Their findings are called the "Yerkes–Dodson law," and they hold true today, more than a century later.

Robert M. Yerkes was one of the first big-time intelligence researchers and a president of the American Psychological Association. He was also a big-time racist and used his own flawed intelligence tests to argue against immigration.

Imagine you're in the thick of a video game battle. Swords are swinging, mobs popping up everywhere and health bars draining dangerously fast.

"Sweetheart," your mom says from the doorway, "don't forget to ..."

You hammer a final button, kill the boss and celebrate a major victory!

But later that day, you're in major trouble. Your mom reminded you to buy milk. But you were immersed in the battle, and you entirely forgot. Or did you? Stress interferes with memory, but it more often interferes with forming memories. When you're in an intense situation, your brain doesn't bother to absorb minor milk-buying details.

Short blasts of stress can impair memory formation. Long-term stress can interfere with brain-cell growth and communication, making it harder to create new memories and retrieve old ones. But scientists at Berkeley University in California have shown that stress can also boost our abilities.

It turns out that under short-term stress, we release a protein called fibroblast growth factor 2. While it doesn't have a catchy name, it does have an interesting purpose. The protein helps new nerve cells to grow in the hippocampi, the areas responsible for memory. (If you used your hippocampi, you might remember it from Chapter 3.)

Researchers put rats in small cages for a few hours to stress them out. They noted the release of extra proteins. Then they measured the rats' mental abilities. A couple of days after the stress, there was no change. But two weeks later, the rats that had endured stress were smarter than their more relaxed relatives.

It sort of makes sense. If you wander into a forest cave, find a black bear hibernating there and run for your life, you need to remember not to re-enter that cave. In fact, you might need some new brain cells to help you think twice about entering *any* cave.

It might even work if it's a video-game cave and a virtual bear.

(Sorry about the milk, Mom.)

"I'm under attack!"

When your immune system gets that signal, it leaps into action. Normally, you have cells called leukocytes circling through your blood and organs. They're like soldiers on guard duty, watching for trouble. The fight-or-flight reaction acts like a giant alarm bell. Extra, off-duty leukocytes pour from your spleen and other resting places. They march quickly through the bloodstream to their battle stations — all the places you might get injured. Some get ready to protect your skin. Others protect your digestive organs, lungs, liver and lymph nodes. All of this happens in a few short seconds.

Scientists have shown that quick bursts of stress can significantly boost your immunity. Your skin becomes better at fighting off infection. The extra immune cells might even fight off tumors. One study showed that a little stress during UV-light exposure could help people resist skin-cancer growth.

So, while long-term, chronic stress is bad for your health, short bursts of stress can be a good thing. That's one reason why exercise is so important. When you play an intense game of soccer, your body pumps with all the good kinds of stress hormones and immune cells. Researchers believe this keeps your immune system in good working order, helping you fight off infection, disease and even cancer.

The more researchers learn about the link between fight-or-flight and the immune system, the more they want to know. Can stress be harnessed? Some people are too sick to play soccer. But if researchers can find a drug or a behavior that triggers the immune-boosting effects of stress, they might be able to help sick people heal more quickly.

 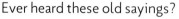

Tough Enough

Ever heard these old sayings?

When the going gets tough, the tough get going.
Tough it out!
Suck it up!

Are any of these adages true? British scientists studied hundreds of athletes between the ages of sixteen and forty-five and found that those with high mental toughness — the ones most committed, confident and in control of their lives — coped better with pressure. Instead of avoiding issues or getting upset, they focused on problem-solving. Other researchers found the same thing in Switzerland: tougher students were less likely to burn out under stress.

So toughness helps with stress. But can stress help with toughness, too?

We explored the idea of post-traumatic growth in Chapter 3, so we know some people use crises as turning points and manage to change their lives or the lives of those around them. We also know (thanks to those lab rats who learned from experience) that a certain amount of stress can make us smarter.

Researchers have put this knowledge to work in practical ways.

Psychologists at the University of Toronto, for example, are using stress research to revamp police training. Assistant professor Judith Andersen puts officers through intense simulations, such as shootings or hostage-takings. She measures officers' stress responses and then creates individualized plans to help them function under pressure. Officers practice making good decisions in the midst of loud noises, while facing large crowds or under time pressure. Those who finish her program are better able to assess situations and judge when to use force.

Judith's work started with the Peel Regional Police in Ontario. She's now collaborating with police forces across Canada, the United States and Europe.

Most of us will never be involved in a shoot-out or a hostage-taking. But it's good to know that we can learn from stressful situations, that we can put stress to use and that, while tough times don't *always* make us stronger, they have the potential to do so.

Stress Busters

Sometimes, stress gets out of control and we need outside help. But for everyday science tests, soccer playoffs and friendship friction, there are lots of ways to make pressure work for you instead of against you.

Get excited. When we let stress amp us up instead of freak us out, we perform better ... in everything from piano recitals to power plays.

Choose your battles. We're at our best when we're confident that our skills match the challenges we face. While a ton of pressure can overwhelm us, a little bit of stress can help us get in the zone.

Get a move on. Exercise creates short bursts of stress hormones that help keep our immune systems ready for action.

Learn from mistakes. You messed up. But guess what? So did lots of those police officers in their training simulations. Make like an officer and learn from your blunders. Figure out what you can do differently next time.

Chapter 5

Tension Tamers

Why couldn't the bicycle stand up by itself?
  It was too tired.
  You probably thought your dad's jokes were just plain annoying. It turns out they're medicinal! Laughter is one of the everyday stress busters getting extra attention from scientists these days, along with other activities like meditation and exercise.

For people dealing with serious anxiety or with stress-related conditions like PTSD, there is a range of therapy options, such as medication and counseling. But what about the rest of us? What about the soccer goalie whose palms sweat before each big game or the science fair genius who can't stop stuttering in front of the judges?

This chapter delves into anti-stress science and the methods regular people around the world use to combat their cortisol. In Japan, workers take walks in the woods — something they call *shinrin yoku*, or forest bathing (read more about this in Going Green on page 66). Harvard Medical School doctors have proven that meditation physically changes the brain, and University of Colorado researchers believe the ability to find humor in tough situations can actually boost our resilience. So from forest trails to comedy hours, this chapter's your guide to all things chill.

Clowning Around

As kids prepare for minor surgery in Lisbon, Portugal, they wait with their parents in standard hospital rooms, cared for by the usual assortment of doctors, nurses ... and clowns.

Researchers there discovered that when clowns were around to help with pre-surgery jitters, kids worried less — and their parents worried less, too. Surprisingly, kids continued to feel less anxious post-surgery, long after the clowns had gone home.

Organized by Operation Red Nose, a professional association of clown "doctors," the performers are specially trained in improvisation and circus skills, as well as in hospital routines and the needs of vulnerable children. They work in eight hospitals throughout the country.

Doctors and scientists in other parts of the world are also recognizing the effects of stress-fighting giggle fits. Humor is free. It doesn't need special facilities or equipment. And it might have the same benefits as much more expensive stress treatments. Initial studies have shown that laughter helps people release anti-stress endorphins, strengthens the immune system and decreases blood pressure.

For older kids and adults, doctors might suggest "laughter therapy" instead of clowns. In a laughter therapy group, people begin by forcing their chuckles. Soon, though, a group's giggles become real.

At the University of Colorado, a professor named Peter McGraw runs a lab entirely devoted to humor. He and his researchers studied humorous responses to Hurricane Sandy, the storm that devastated the northeast coast of the United States in 2012.

Wait ... humorous responses to a deadly storm? Doesn't that seem strange? It's true that hurricane jokes *during* the disaster could be considered offensive. But scientists found that the same sorts of jokes became funny shortly after the danger had passed (sort of like sticking out your tongue at a bully *after* he's out of sight). A few wry comments and headshaking chuckles accomplished two unique things: they helped people feel strong enough to cope with loss and form supportive friendships. Humor was a tool people used to get through a stressful time.

So how many laughs should a doctor prescribe? Are comedy videos better than clowns? Can humor promote physical healing as well as mental well-being? The research has just begun. Doctors and scientists are investigating these exact questions, in hopes that laughter might actually be the best medicine.

Screen Screams

The babysitter hears a noise from the basement. Ignoring the storm raging outside and the organ playing in the background, she tiptoes down the creaky stairs. A shadow looms on the wall ...

AHHHH!

Some people swear that horror movies help them blow off steam. But the makers of suspense films don't set out to decrease stress — they want to freak people out! Since the 1940s, filmmakers have been exploiting our imaginations

by suggesting that threatening things are happening just offscreen. From our theater seats, we notice strange noises. We see flickers of movement. We grow tense and uneasy. Suddenly ... BANG! Our popcorn goes flying as we leap straight into fight-or-flight mode.

Does that short-term stress have benefits? Maybe. Researchers in Britain tested people's blood after a screening of *The Texas Chainsaw Massacre*. The results proved that the stress and the accompanying adrenaline rush gave viewers a short-term immune system boost.

But when we're attacked, our bodies also release extra chemicals to combat bleeding. A Dutch study found that by triggering those chemicals, horror-movie scares significantly increased the risk of dangerous blood clots, which can lead to a stroke or a heart attack. (It seems "bloodcurdling screams" can be real.)

So ... should you see a horror movie to relieve stress? Only if your heart's in good shape!

Ever dream of guinea pig intestines? Hans Walter Kosterlitz did, and it led to a major discovery.

Here's the experiment he dreamed about and later performed: he gave a strip of guinea pig intestine a small electric zap. The muscles in the intestine contracted. Then he added opiates — the powerful drugs derived from opium poppies — and gave the intestine another zap. The muscles no longer contracted.

With this 1975 experiment, Hans became one of the people who helped discover opiate receptors.

Your nervous system communicates by sending signals between nerve cells. An opiate receptor is a little receiver on the surface of some of these cells. Once a certain type of drug molecule binds to that receiver, it blocks the pathway for pain signals. That's why a surgeon might prescribe an opiate such as morphine after an operation — the drug will bind to nerve-cell receptors and block pain.

The discovery of these microscopic receivers got scientists thinking. Poppies first grew in the Mediterranean and Middle East, so not all early humans were exposed to opium. But people from all ethnic groups have opiate receptors. How is that possible? There must be some sort of naturally occurring drug inside our heads.

Sure enough, a few years later, they discovered the first of these chemicals.

In our bodies, there are endogenous, or

internal, morphine molecules. Scientists have nicknamed them "endorphins." And they're powerful. Like morphine, they can block pain signals inside our brains and give us a blast of happiness.

We all know to "just say no" to drugs. *Except* when those "drugs" are naturally occurring chemicals produced by our own glands and nervous systems!

Ride the Rush

Maybe you're training for a marathon. Your friend thinks that's just crazy.

"Are you on drugs?" she says.

Well, kind of! Exercise is one of the most effective stress-relievers because when we push ourselves through intense activity, our bodies release endorphins. That's why people talk of a "runner's high" or an "endorphin rush."

Exercise has other stress-busting benefits, too. Volleyball, yoga, tennis, standing on one foot while juggling bowling pins — any kind of physical activity helps our hearts, lungs, muscles and nervous systems work smoothly together. The better our systems cooperate, the better we are at achieving *homeostasis*. That's the word Walter Cannon (the cat food guy from Chapter 1) coined way back in 1926. It means having all our systems in balance.

There's a third stress-busting benefit to exercise. Often, we play sports on teams, we meet friends for a jog or we gather together for yoga classes. Social interaction is one of the best antidotes for pressure.

So, gather your friends, get your systems in order and get high together — an all-natural, brain-induced runner's high, that is.

Pal Power

Co-rumination. It sounds like what a cow does after eating too much, but it's actually science speak for "gossip." Research has shown that people with supportive friends have lower cortisol levels. Great friendships make life less stressful. On the other hand, groups of friends that hash over sad stories and focus on negative news — groups that co-ruminate — can actually increase stress levels.

As Serena Williams stands at the baseline, ready to serve, she bounces her tennis ball exactly five times. It's a pregame ritual, and Serena's not the only tennis player to have one. Before Rafael Nadal serves, he adjusts his shirt, wipes his nose, pushes his hair behind his ears ... and picks his underwear out of his butt.

His underwear can't possibly slide out of place that often. So what's going on?

Researchers in Germany set out to study these random acts. They found that tennis players who learn pregame rituals play significantly better under pressure. While their cortisol levels remain the same, they *feel* better able to cope and their performances improve. Other studies show similar results among golfers; gymnasts; and football, basketball and soccer players. Those with pregame routines are least likely to choke under stress.

Most rituals include cues that remind the athlete to breathe, focus and visualize success.

Not everyone needs a ritual, though. Researchers have found these routines especially useful for those who get serious pregame jitters. (Also, not everyone wants to butt-pick in public.)

A Side Order of Stress

One bag of barbecue-flavored potato chips.
One large bowl of macaroni and cheese.
One double helping of chocolate cheesecake.

While no dietician would recommend that menu, many of us reach for oozy, salty, sugary comfort foods in times of stress. Why? For years, people have assumed that the pleasure of delicious food helps us balance the pain of a difficult situation.

Then scientists in Switzerland chowed down on years of research. In 2015, they came up with an alternate theory: Under pressure, we abandon our regular goals and decision-making strategies. We rely on triggers and habits instead. Is that the crinkle of a tinfoil bag? Eat chips! Did the clock just strike midnight? Midnight snack!

It's possible we're not even enjoying our buckets of ice cream. Several studies have shown that under stress, we're less able to respond to pleasure. Our brains are too busy. So while we're driven to *want* comfort food, we don't actually *like* it as much as we would in calmer times.

The Swiss researchers have a solution, and it doesn't come with a side of fries. They suggest that people facing high levels of stress "regulate the food environment." In other words, leave the cake at the grocery store and the sugared cereal in the cupboard. By reducing the number of triggers around us, we're less likely to accidentally eat our feelings.

Amping It Up

It's already midnight, but you have to finish your science project. There's no time for sleep. Should you reach for an energy drink?

While the drink might help you feel more awake (at least temporarily), you're actually increasing your stress. Caffeine stimulates the nervous system, boosts cortisol and adrenaline levels and increases blood pressure — just as stress does. In the short term, combining stress and caffeine might give you a bad case of jitters. In the long term, it can cause overeating, mess with your sleep and weaken your immune system.

The Dream Team

Did you hear "sleep" and "stress" confirmed their relationship status on Facebook?

It's complicated.

A good night's sleep can counteract stress. Scientists believe that during the deepest levels of sleep, the human body works to regulate cortisol. It's as if a cleanup crew whisks through your bloodstream, sweeping away extra stress hormones.

There's just one problem: stress can cause poor sleep. With higher cortisol levels, we have trouble getting to sleep and staying asleep, and we're more likely to have nightmares. Even when we do nod off, we don't achieve the same quality of rest.

So ... we need sleep to deal with stress, but stress makes it harder to sleep. What are we supposed to do? Lie awake, knowing our insomnia will make our worries even worse? For most of us, the answer is simply time. More time to sleep, more time for our worries to pass, more time for exam periods or sports playoffs to end and for life to get back to normal. A few days of droopy eyelids won't spell disaster. However, the sleep/stress research is important for those suffering from extreme anxiety or PTSD. If doctors and therapists can help those people sleep better, healing might come sooner.

Getting Your "Om" On

Focus on your breath. When a thought arises, notice and acknowledge that thought, then let it go. Bring yourself back to the sensation of the breath.

Is this a yoga session or a fifth-grade classroom?

It could be either! Many teachers are embracing meditation and mindfulness as antidotes to school stress. *Meditation* means focusing on breath, sensation or sound for an extended period of time. *Mindfulness* means focusing on the present moment, without judging or reacting.

Teachers use these techniques in different ways. In some classrooms, students spend several quiet minutes in meditation after the morning and lunchtime bells. Others teach specific mindfulness techniques that students can use anywhere. Kids might pause before a test, for example, to focus on their breathing, scan their bodies for stress and notice — but not judge — their emotions.

In adults, researchers have used brain scans to show how meditation activates areas associated with memory and empathy and soothes areas associated with stress. Remember the amygdalae, those almond-shaped fight-or-flight control rooms in our brains? A 2012 American study found that meditation caused physical changes in the amygdalae. Thanks to those changes, beginner meditation students showed better focus and better emotional control.

Those types of brain scans haven't been done on kids. But studies in Britain have shown that students who practice meditation are better at ignoring distractions and suffer less from stress and depression.

Scientists at Oxford University and University College London have embarked on a much larger enterprise that involves seven thousand teenagers. For seven years, some

Find Five

Want to try a mindfulness exercise? Take a few deep, slow breaths, and then try this one: Look at five things in the room, listen for four things, then touch three things. Next, look for four things, listen for three, and touch two. Repeat the process, doing fewer each time.

of those teens will meditate, while others will go about life as usual. With brain scans, computerized tests and real-life results, researchers hope to judge once and for all whether meditation can boost mental health.

You could stay tuned for a decade and see what those researchers decide. Or you could give mindfulness a try and see for yourself. There are plenty of books, YouTube videos and apps to help beginners get Zen.

Going Green

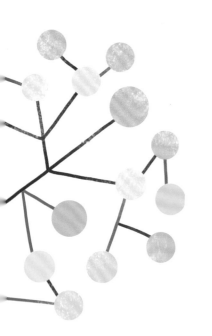

Immerse yourself in nature — you'll feel better. That's what Japan's Director of Forestry told the country's overwhelmed workers in 1982. He coined the term *shinrin yoku*, or "forest bathing." The idea was to absorb the forest using all the body's senses.

Was it true? Could walking in the woods decrease stress?

Yoshifumi Miyazaki set out to find proof. His first study showed that patients who walked through a forest had lower cortisol levels than those who walked around a lab. Next, he sent 744 participants to 62 forests all across Japan. Teams of researchers tested the participants' cortisol levels, blood pressure, heart rates and sympathetic nervous system activation. Again and again, the results came back positive. Forests drained away anxiety and boosted well-being. After only fifteen minutes among the trees, people's cortisol levels dropped more than 13 percent.

Even more studies followed. Forest bathing helped people with high blood pressure, diabetes and weak immune systems.

Outside of Japan, other scientists began to take notice. Soon, positive findings poured in from around the world. In North America, researchers found that kids who spent more time in nature had better test scores and self-discipline. Those with attention-deficit/hyperactivity disorder (ADHD) had fewer behavioral problems.

Why is *shinrin yoku* so stress-busting? Yoshifumi says it's because, for millions of years, we lived surrounded by trees instead of cars and computers. Our bodies are designed to respond to nature. Research seems to support his theory. Here are just a few of the nature-based things proven to reduce blood pressure or help the immune system:

- the scent of wood oils
- views of flowers or plants
- the feel of cypress or cedar

And ... great news! We don't need a whole forest to reap the stress-busting benefits of nature. Science shows that a walk in a city park can be exactly what the nature-doctor ordered.

Stress Busters

It's conclusive! Everyday activities can counteract the negative effects of stress and help us chill out.

Get giggling. Gather your friends for a comedy flick or read a joke book.

Pump it up. Intense exercise will flood your body with pain-blocking endorphins. Any kind of exercise will boost your immunity. Even better: exercise with friends.

Find Zen. Download a meditation app, join a yoga class or read a book about mindfulness. After a few weeks, see if you feel more relaxed.

Go back to nature. A walk in the park or a hike in the woods is one of the best-researched ways to shed stress.

Conclusion

Personal Space

Stress research has gone microscopic. Each year, scientists learn more about our hormones, our genes and our brain cells. But stress research has also gone big. In fact, it's blasted right into outer space.

In 2015, scientists asked American astronaut Scott Kelly to assemble a 3D cube to match a particular pattern — sort of like completing a Rubik's Cube. Next, he was asked to do the same thing after eating freeze-dried food, sleeping poorly and listening to constant noise — for a year. Oh, and while orbiting 400 km (250 mi.) above Earth.

From March 2015 to March 2016, Scott Kelly and Russian cosmonaut Mikhail Kornienko lived aboard the International Space Station. They spent twice the usual amount of time up there, all so scientists could test how the human body and brain react to months and months of chronic stress. Researchers already knew that astronauts faced plenty of problems: loneliness, wacky light/dark cycles, heavy workloads, droning engine noise and weird physical changes. (Did you know that people's eyeballs change shape in space?) They also understood that under long-term stress, the human brain can have issues with mood, sleep and focus. They wanted to know if that happened the same way in space.

It's an important question as scientists prepare for the first human missions to Mars. It will take astronauts 150 to 300 days to reach the red planet. Can you imagine if you and your friends were locked in a small space together for that long? There would probably be friction! Plus, there are possible mechanical, health and safety challenges to consider. Heading to another planet for the very first time might get a wee bit stressful!

Scott and Mikhail served as low-gravity guinea pigs. For the entire year, they wore wristbands to monitor their sleep, wrote journal entries to track their moods and hooked their brains to MRI scanners while they worked on puzzle after puzzle. Scientists watched how the men's brains began to literally rewire themselves to adapt to the tasks and the environment.

Scott and Mikhail are back on Earth now, but they're still doing puzzles. It will take a few more years for researchers to decide exactly how they dealt with stress, how their brains changed and whether those changes were reversed once gravity was restored. Eventually, NASA will use that information to help train Mars travelers.

Meanwhile, the researchers are applying NASA's early findings to other extreme environments. They think these space-based experiments might help scientists in the Arctic or soldiers in the desert keep their emotional cool. After all, there's plenty of extreme stress right here on Earth, and plenty more for stress researchers to discover.

Further Reading

Becker, Helaine. *Don't Stress: How to Handle Life's Little Problems*. Toronto: Scholastic, 2016.

Morgan, Nicola. *The Teenage Guide to Stress*. London: Walker Books, 2014.

Reber, Deborah. *Chill: Stress-Reducing Techniques for a More Balanced, Peaceful You*. New York: Simon Pulse, 2015.

Shannon, Jennifer. *The Anxiety Survival Guide for Teens: CBT Skills to Overcome Fear, Worry and Panic*. Oakland: Instant Help, 2015.

Verde, Susan. *I Am Peace: A Book of Mindfulness*. New York: Abrams Books for Young Readers, 2017.

Wells, Polly. *Freaking Out: Real-Life Stories About Anxiety*. Toronto: Annick Press, 2013.

Selected Sources

Chapter 1

"Bureau d'Énquêtes et d'Analyses pour la sécurité de l'aviation civile. Final Report: On the Accident on 1st June 2009 to the Airbus A330-203 registered F-GZCP operated by Air France flight AF 447 Rio de Janeiro–Paris. Published July 2012. Accessed January 30, 2017. https://www.bea.aero/docspa/2009/f-cp090601.en/pdf/f-cp090601.en.pdf

Cannon, Walter. *Bodily Changes in Pain, Hunger, Fear and Rage: An Account of Recent Researches into the Function of Emotional Excitement*. New York: D. Appleton and Company, 1915.

Davis, A.K. "Lifting Capacity of Horned Passalus Beetles During Passive and Stressed States." *Journal of Insect Behavior*, 2014, pp. 496–502.

Enoka, Roger. "Involuntary Muscle Contractions and the Unintentional Discharge of a Firearm." *Law Enforcement Executive Forum*, 2003, pp. 27–40.

Feinstein, Justin S., et al. "The Human Amygdala and the Induction and Experience of Fear." *Current Biology*, January 2012, pp. 34–38.

Fenz, Walter D., and Seymour Epstein. "Gradients of Physiological Arousal in Parachutists as a Function of an Approaching Jump." *Psychosomatic Medicine*, January 1967, pp. 33–51.

Galassi, Francesco M., et al. "Fight-or-Flight Response in the Ancient Egyptian Novel 'Sinuhe.'" *Autonomic Neuroscience*, February 2016, pp. 27–28.

Gwirtz, Patricia A. "Teaching the Interrelationship Between Stress, Emotions, and Cardiovascular Risk Using a Classic Paper by Walter Cannon." *Advances in Physiology Education*, March 1, 2008, pp. 18–22.

Heim, Christopher, et al. "The Risk of Involuntary Firearms Discharge." *Human Factors*, September 2006, pp. 413–421.

Martin, Wayne L., et al. "Fear-Potentiated Startle: A Review from an Aviation Perspective." *The International Journal of Aviation Psychology*. April 2015, pp. 97–107.

Chapter 2

"American Psychological Association Survey Shows Teen Stress Rivals That of Adults." From the website of the American Psychological Association. Published February 11, 2014. Accessed February 3, 2017. http://www.apa.org/news/press/releases/2014/02/teen-stress.aspx

Bangasser, D.A. "Sex Differences in Stress-Related Receptors: 'Micro' Differences with 'Macro' Implications for Mood and Anxiety Disorders." *Biology of Sex Differences*, January 21, 2013.

———"Stress." *Scientific American Mind*, November 2016, p. 58.

Cadwalladr, Carole. "Nepal Earthquake: British Doctor Saved 23 Lives after Everest Avalanche." *Guardian* (UK edition), May 9, 2015.

Fleck, Fiona. "Carlo Urbani." *British Medical Journal*, 2003, p. 825.

Iserson, Kenneth V., et al. "Fight or Flight: The Ethics of Emergency Physician Disaster Response." *Annals of Emergency Medicine*, April 2008, pp. 345–353.

Lau, B. W. K. "Does the Stress in Childhood and Adolescence Matter? A Psychological Perspective." *Perspectives in Public Health*, 2002, pp. 238–244.

Lee, M., and R. Larson. "The Korean 'Examination Hell': Long Hours of Studying, Distress, and Depression." *Journal of Youth and Adolescence*, 2000, pp. 249–271.

Oberle, Eva, and Kimberly A. Schonert-Reichl. "Stress Contagion in the Classroom?: The Link Between Classroom Teacher Burnout and Morning Cortisol in Elementary School Students." *Social Science & Medicine*, 2016, pp. 30–37.

"One-third of Ontario Students Report Elevated Psychological Distress, CAMH Survey Shows." From the website of the Centre for Addiction and Mental Health. Published July 21, 2016. Accessed February 3, 2017. http://www.camh.ca/en/hospital/about_camh/newsroom/news_releases_media_advisories_and_backgrounders/current_year/Pages/One-third-of-Ontario-students-report-elevated-psychological-distress.aspx

Palmer, L., et al. "The Relationship Between Stress, Fatigue, and Cognitive Functioning." *College Student Journal*, Spring 2014, p. 198.

Shapero, B., et al. "Interaction of Biological Stress Recovery and Cognitive Vulnerability for Depression in Adolescence." *Journal of Youth and Adolescence*, January 2017, p. 91.

Starcke, Katrin, and Matthias Brand. "Decision Making Under Stress: A Selective Review." *Neuroscience & Biobehavioral Reviews*. April 2012, pp. 1228–1248.

Chapter 3

Arpawong, T.E., et al. "Post-Traumatic Growth among an Ethnically Diverse Sample of Adolescent and Young Adult Cancer Survivors." *Psycho-Oncology*, October 2013, pp. 2235–2244.

García, Felipe E., and Anna Wlodarczyk. "Psychometric Properties of the Posttraumatic Growth Inventory—Short Form Among Chilean Adults." *Journal of Loss and Trauma*, July 2016, pp. 303–314.

Matson, H. "The Treatment of 'Shell Shock' in World War I: Early Attitudes and Treatments for Post-Traumatic Stress Disorder and Combat Stress Reaction." *European Psychiatry*, March 2016, pp. S636.

Matsumura, Janice. "State Propaganda and Mental Disorders: The Issue of Psychiatric Casualties among Japanese Soldiers During the Asia-Pacific War." *Bulletin of the History of Medicine*, December 2004, pp. 804–835.

McGonigal, Kelly. *The Upside of Stress: Why Stress Is Good for You and How to Get Good at It*. New York: Penguin Random House, 2015.

Morley, Christopher A., and Brandon A. Kohrt. "Impact of Peer Support on PTSD, Hope and Functional Impairment: A Mixed-Methods Study of Child Soldiers in Nepal." *Journal of Aggression, Maltreatment and Trauma*, August 2013, pp. 714–734.

Pitman, Roger K. "Biological Studies of Post-Traumatic Stress Disorder." *Nature Reviews Neuroscience*, November 2012, pp. 769.

"Program History" from the website of Warrior Canine Connection. Accessed May 29, 2017. http://www.warriorcanineconnection.org/how-we-help-warriors/history/

Stern, Stephen L., et al. "Potential Benefits of Canine Companionship for Military Veterans with Posttraumatic Stress Disorder (PTSD)." *Society & Animals*, 2013, pp. 568–581.

Storr, Will. "Kony's Child Soldiers: When You Kill for the First Time, You Change." *Telegraph* (UK), February 12, 2014.

Taylor, Shelley E. "Tend and Befriend: Biobehavioral Bases of Affiliation under Stress." *Current Directions in Psychological Science*, December 2006, pp. 273–277.

Taylor, Shelley E., et al. "Behavioral Responses to Stress in Females: Tend-and-Befriend, Not Fight-or-Flight." *Psychological Review*, July 2000, pp. 411–429.

van der Kolk, Bessel A., et al. "A Randomized Controlled Study of Neurofeedback for Chronic PTSD." *PLoS One*, December 2016.

Yehuda, Rachel, and Linda M. Bierer. "The Relevance of Epigenetics to PTSD: Implications for the DSM-V." *Journal of Traumatic Stress*, October 2009, pp. 427–434.

Zhao, Changyi, et al. "The Association between Post-Traumatic Stress Disorder Symptoms and the Quality of Life among Wenchuan Earthquake Survivors: The Role of Social Support as a Moderator." *Quality of Life Research*, 2013, pp. 733–743.

Chapter 4

Andersen, Judith P., and Harri Gustafsberg. "A Training Method to Improve Police Use of Force Decision Making." *SAGE Open*, April 2016.

Brooks, Alison Wood. "Get Excited: Reappraising Pre-Performance Anxiety as Excitement." *Journal of Experimental Psychology*, June 1, 2014, pp. 1144–1158.

Carney, Dana R., et al. "Power Posing: Brief, Nonverbal Displays Affect Neuroendochrine Levels and Risk Tolerance." *Psychological Science*, October 2010, pp. 1363–1368.

Dhabhar, Firdaus S. "Effects of Stress on Immune Function: The Good, the Bad, and the Beautiful." *Immunologic Research*, May 2014, pp. 193–210.

Fricchione, Gregory L., Ana Ivkovic and Albert S. Yeung. *The Science of Stress: Living Under Pressure*. Chicago: The University of Chicago Press, 2016.

Jones, Marc, et al. "A Theory of Challenge and Threat States in Athletes." *International Review of Sport and Exercise Psychology*, September 2009, pp. 161–180.

Kaiseler, Mariana, et al. "Mental Toughness, Stress, Stress Appraisal, Coping and Coping Effectiveness in Sport." *Personality and Individual Differences*, 2009, pp. 728–733.

Kirby, Elizabeth D., et al. "Acute Stress Enhances Adult Rat Hippocampal Neurogenesis and Activation of Newborn Neurons via Secreted Astrocytic FGF2." *eLife*, 2013. Accessed May 15, 2017.

McGonigal, Kelly. *The Upside of Stress: Why Stress Is Good for You, and How to Get Good at It*. New York: Penguin Random House, 2015.

Monasterio, Erik, et al. "Personality Characteristics of BASE Jumpers." *Journal of Applied Sport Psychology*, February 2012, pp. 391–400.

Monasterio, Erik, et al. "Stress Reactivity and Personality in Extreme Sport Athletes: The Psychobiology of BASE Jumpers." *Physiology & Behavior*, December 2016, pp. 289–297.

Sezgin, A. Ufuk, and Raija-Leena Punamäki. "Perceived Changes in Social Relations after Earthquake Trauma among Eastern Anatolian Women: Associated Factors and Mental Health Consequences." *Stress and Health*, December 16, 2014, pp. 355–366.

Teicher, Jeremy. "For Alexi Pappas, Nightmares Mean You Care." *New York Times*, July 20, 2016.

Tozman, Tahmine, et al. "Inverted U-Shaped Function Between Flow and Cortisol Release During Chess Play." *Journal of Happiness Studies*, February 1, 2017, pp. 247–268.

Zhao, Changyi, et al. "The Association between Post Traumatic Stress Disorder Symptoms and the Quality of Life among Wenchuan Earthquake Survivors: The Role of Social Support as a Moderator." *Quality of Life Research*, May 2013, pp. 733–743.

Chapter 5

Booth, Robert. "Mindfulness Study to Track Effect of Meditation on 7,000 Teenagers." *Guardian* (UK edition), July 15, 2015.

Byrd-Craven, Jennifer, et al. "Stress Reactivity to Co-Rumination in Young Women's Friendships." *Journal of Social and Personal Relationships*, June 2011, p. 469.

Desbordes, Gaëlle G., et al. "Effects of Mindful-Attention and Compassion Meditation Training on Amygdala Response to Emotional Stimuli in an Ordinary, Non-Meditative State." *Frontiers in Human Neuroscience*, 2012, p. 292.

Fernandes, Sara Costa, and Patrícia Arriaga. "The Effects of Clown Intervention on Worries and Emotional Responses in Children Undergoing Surgery." *Journal of Health Psychology*, April 2010, pp. 405–415.

Gu, Jenny, et al. "How Do Mindfulness-Based Cognitive Therapy and Mindfulness-Based Stress Reduction Improve Mental Health and Wellbeing?: A Systematic Review and Meta-Analysis of Mediation Studies." *Clinical Psychology Review*, November 2016, p. 119.

Lautenbach, Franziska, et al. "Nonautomated Pre-Performance Routine in Tennis: An Intervention Study." *Journal of Applied Sport Psychology*, April 2015, pp. 123–131.

McGraw, A., et al. "The Rise and Fall of Humor: Psychological Distance Modulates Humorous Responses to Tragedy." *Social Psychological and Personality Science*, July 2014, pp. 566–572.

Mesagno, Christopher, and Thomas Mullane-Grant. "A Comparison of Different Pre-Performance Routines as Possible Choking Interventions." *Journal of Applied Sport Psychology*, July 2010, pp. 343–360.

Mian, Rubina, et al. "Observing a Fictitious Stressful Event: Haematological Changes Including Circulating Leukocyte Activation." *The International Journal on the Biology of Stress*, 2003, pp. 41–47.

Mohino-Herranz, Inma, et al. "Assessment of Mental, Emotional and Physical Stress through Analysis of Physiological Signals Using Smartphones." *Sensors*, October 2015, pp. 25607–25627.

Nemeth, Banne, et al. "Bloodcurdling Movies and Measures of Coagulation: Fear Factor Crossover Trial." *British Medical Journal*, 2015.

Routhier-Martin, Kayli, et al. "Exploring Mindfulness and Meditation for the Elementary Classroom: Intersections Across Current Multidisciplinary Research." *Childhood Education*, March 2017, pp. 168–175.

Seltenrich, Nate. "Just What the Doctor Ordered: Using Parks to Improve Children's Health." *Environmental Health Perspectives*, October 2015, p. A254.

Song, Chorong, Harumi Ikei and Yoshifumi Miyazaki. "Physiological Effects of Nature Therapy: A Review of the Research in Japan." *International Journal of Environmental Research and Public Health*, August 2016, pp. 1–17.

Conclusion

"Don't Stress the Small Stuff: NASA's One-Year Mission Research Helps Combat Stress and Fatigue." Published June 8, 2015; Last updated August 6, 2017. Accessed January 31, 2017. https://www.nasa.gov/content/dont-stress-the-small-stuff-nasa-1ym-research-helps-combat-stress-and-fatigue

Index

abuse, 29, 33
addiction, 19, 20
adrenal glands, 9
adrenaline, 9, 18, 34, 44, 47, 59
Afghanistan, 33, 36
Air France, 12–13
American Civil War, 32
American Psychological Association, 20, 29
amygdalae, 8, 21, 65
Andersen, Judith, 54–55
art therapy, 20
astronauts, 68–69
athletes, 16, 46–47, 48–49, 53, 62
autonomic nervous system, 9

Betancourt, Theresa, 38–39
blood pressure, 57, 66
brain-computer interaction devices, 36
Brooks, Alison Wood, 45–46

cancer, 43
Cannon, Walter, 7, 9, 61
challenge state, 47, 49
chemicals, 4, 9, 17, 59, 61
    See also hormones
child soldiers, 31
    See also Okello, Norman
Chile, 42
China, 40
chronic stress, 5, 15, 17, 18–29, 68–69
clowns, 57
cortisol, 9, 21, 34, 39, 46, 47, 49, 56, 61, 62, 64, 66
co-rumination, 61
counselors, 21, 29, 35, 43, 56

depression, 19, 21, 27, 34, 35
    See also mental health
Diagnostic and Statistical Manual of Mental Disorders, 32
dissociation, 34
DNA. See genes
doctors, 21, 23–24, 26, 43, 58
    See also Tullet, Rachel; Urbani, Carlo
Doctors Without Borders, 22–23
Dodson, John Dillingham, 49

earthquakes, 40–41, 42
eating disorders, 19
endorphins, 44, 57, 61
Enoka, Roger, 11
epigenetics, 38
Epstein, Seymour, 16
exercise, 29, 53, 55, 56, 61, 67
    See also athletes

fear, 7, 15
Fenz, Walter, 16
fight-or-flight response, 5, 6–17, 18, 21, 33, 39–41, 44, 46, 53
fight, flight or freeze, 7
firefighters, 19, 26
flashbacks, 34
flow state, 49
friendship, 4, 21, 30, 31, 39, 40–41, 43, 55, 61

gender, 27–28, 39–41
genes, 27–29, 34, 38, 68

heart disease, 14–15, 18, 19, 59
hippocampi, 34, 51
Hodes, Georgia E., 27–28
homeostasis, 61

homework, 20–21, 47
hormones, 4, 9, 15, 17, 18–19, 34, 37, 48, 49, 64, 68
    See also adrenaline, cortisol, endorphins, oxytocin
horned beetles, 12
horror movies, 58–59
humor, 56–58, 67

immune system, 10, 19, 52–53, 57, 59, 66
    leukocytes, 52
Iraq, 33, 36

Japan, 56, 66

Kelly, Scott, 68–69
Kornienko, Mikhail, 68–69
Kosterlitz, Hans Walter, 60

laughter. See humor
long-term stress. See chronic stress
Lord's Resistance Army, 31

McGraw, Peter, 58
Médecins Sans Frontières, 22–23
medication, 15, 20, 35, 56
meditation, 21, 35, 56, 65–66, 67
memory, 33, 34, 50–51
mental health, 19, 20–21, 24, 32–36, 53, 58, 66
mindfulness, 21, 67
    in schools, 65
mindset interventions, 46
Miyazaki, Yoshifumi, 66
morphine, 60, 61
Mount Everest, 26–27

Nadal, Rafael, 62

natural disasters, 18
nature, 66–67
nervous system, 9–10, 14, 60
   autonomic nervous
      system, 9
   parasympathetic nervous
      system, 10
   sympathetic nervous
      system, 9, 66
nightmares, 31, 34, 64
norepinephrine, 9
nucleus accumbens, 27

Okello, Norman, 31, 33
opiates, 60
oxytocin, 37, 40

panic attacks, 14–15
Pappas, Alexi, 46–47
paramedics, 19, 26
parasympathetic nervous
      system, 10
pilots, 12–14
police officers, 11–12, 14, 19,
      21, 26
   training, 54–55
Portugal, 57
post-traumatic growth,
      42–43, 54
post-traumatic stress
      disorder (PTSD),
      33–39, 42, 56, 64
prefrontal cortex, 8, 34
psychologists, 29, 32, 33, 49,
      54
   See also counselors

Rwanda, 38–39
resilience, 30, 39, 56

schools, 21, 65
   See also homework
Selye, Hans, 8, 18

Severe Acute Respiratory
      Syndrome (SARS), 22–23
shinrin yoku, 66–67
Sinuhe, 9
sleep, 21, 29, 64
soldiers, 19, 21, 26
   See also child soldiers
sports, 16, 46–47, 48–49, 53,
      61, 62, 64
startle response, 11–12
sympathetic nervous
      system, 9, 66
Szymanski, Mateusz, 28

Taylor, Shelley, 39–40
tend and befriend, 40
therapy animals, 36–37
threat state, 47
trauma, 5, 15, 20, 30–43
Tullet, Rachel, 26–27
Turkey, 41

Uganda, 31
Urbani, Carlo, 22–23

veterans, 32–37
Vietnam, 22–23, 33
Vietnam War, 33

war, 30–33, 39
Warrior Canine Connection,
      36
Williams, Serena, 62
World Health Organization,
      22
World War I, 32
World War II, 33

Yerkes-Dodson law, 49
Yerkes, Robert M., 49
Yount, Rick, 36–37